5 days

5
days

A Lifetime of Love in
Seven Thousand Two Hundred Minutes

Christine Marie Staszesky

5 days: A Lifetime of Love in
Seven Thousand Two Hundred Minutes

Copyright © 2021 by Christin Marie Staszesky

ISBN 978-1-63821-798-5

Book design & layout: Mark Gelotte www.markgelotte.com

First edition printed in May 2021

Printed in the United States of America

To my beloved mom,

Clare-Marie Costantini and to all of us

who have known love and loss and the transformational power of both.

Uncle Rudy, I still miss you.

in loving

there is always a leaving

but if we are lucky

we are left with a love boon

like a sigh

after the setting

of

the

sun

~ the Light Rider

The moment I realized that I have touched
you more this day and yesterday
than I ever have in ten years
of knowing you.

INTRODUCTION

Joseph and I knew each other for ten years. Our relationship was difficult, layered and complex. We often fought. It was always over my mother.

We explored many avenues of healing, although none lasted. Things went on this way, and the years ticked by. The impasse caused us all great pain.

One month prior to his death, something happened. It was my birthday, and in my family we celebrate a tradition called a Swedish Birthday. My mother learned this tradition from an exchange student her family had brought to live with them when she was sixteen. The birthday person is woken up by the family members softly singing happy birthday and bringing with them a tray holding a lit candle, the birthday person's favorite morning beverage, one or two small wrapped presents and a sweet treat.

On this birthday my mother and Joseph sat with me on the large porch of their home in the early morning, sharing the dawn, and the birthday tray mom had thoughtfully prepared for me. After the brief loving festivities, Joseph got up, walked around the small birthday table and stood in front of mom and me.

We looked at each other. His eyes searched for mine and held them. This was highly unusual.

When he spoke, his voice trembled. "Christin, I have a gift for you." He held up his cup of steaming coffee and told me that he had come to a realization. "I am sorry I have wasted so much time. All these years. Fighting. With you. I am finished fighting." I thought I saw tears in his eyes.

He shared some other touching words that I can't remember, although I can still feel them. My mother's face was streaming with tears of joy. I got up and wrapped my arms around him, and sincerely whispered, "Thank you. Me too."

His graciousness healed us both. All the years of arguing and hard words melted away. They were replaced by the delicate bloom of release that true forgiveness from both sides can bring. His apology, which became his parting gift to me, allowed me to not only be willing, but also to want to care for him with attention and tenderness the last five days of his life.

In that moment, we ceased being the estranged stepfather and stepdaughter and became precious parent and precious daughter to each other.

Christin Marie Staszesky
December 2020
Van Vleck, Texas

1

The moment I realized
I wouldn't be going home.

2

The moment I realized
hospice was in the house.

3

The moment I realized that
they would actually be leaving
and we would be in charge of the night.

4

The moment I realized
this would be
just mom and me.
And you.

5

The moment I realized
I would be the one to medicate you.

6

The moment I realized that I have touched
you more this day and yesterday
than I ever have in ten years
of knowing you.

7

The moment I realized
I cared.

8

The moment I realized
I really cared.

9

The moment I realized
I was still in my pajamas.
For the third day in a row.

10

The moment I realized
I was outside for the first time
all day at 7:00 p.m.
Feeding horses.
In my pajamas.

11

The moment I realized
I couldn't do this anymore.

12

The moment I looked up to the sky,
through arms of oaks,
my eyes finding an owl feather.
Suspended in air by a spider string.
Twirling slow.

13

The moment I realized
I **had** to. Keep doing. **This.**

14

This.

Putting one foot in front of the other.

So I did.

15

The moment I realized
I loved you.

16

The moment I realized
I had anointed you, dying man.
With tenderly prepared foot bath.
Salt. Oils. Love.

17

The look of mom's gratitude
from across the room,
seeing me sitting with you
when she had to take a break
to pet the cat, instead of you.

18

The moment we understood
your left lung was completely collapsed,
silent. Already gone.
The other barely allowing air in.

19

It meant you would never lie flat again.

You wouldn't be able to die in your own bed.

In your own room with mom.

We tried so hard to make you comfortable.

We couldn't.

20

You'd never lie down again.

21

We'd lose you sitting up.

22

The moment I realized I wasn't breathing.

23

The moment I realized
I was only listening to your breathing.
Ragged.

24

The moment I asked you,
"Are you scared?"

25

The moment you slowly, barely
turned your head. Left.
Then right.
"No."

26

The moment I realized
you were enjoying our insane
exhaustion-induced-punch-drunk-laughter.
Your eyebrow went up.
Once. Twice.

27

The moment I became your
personal bouncer with visitors.
"Thank you for coming, he's tired now."

28

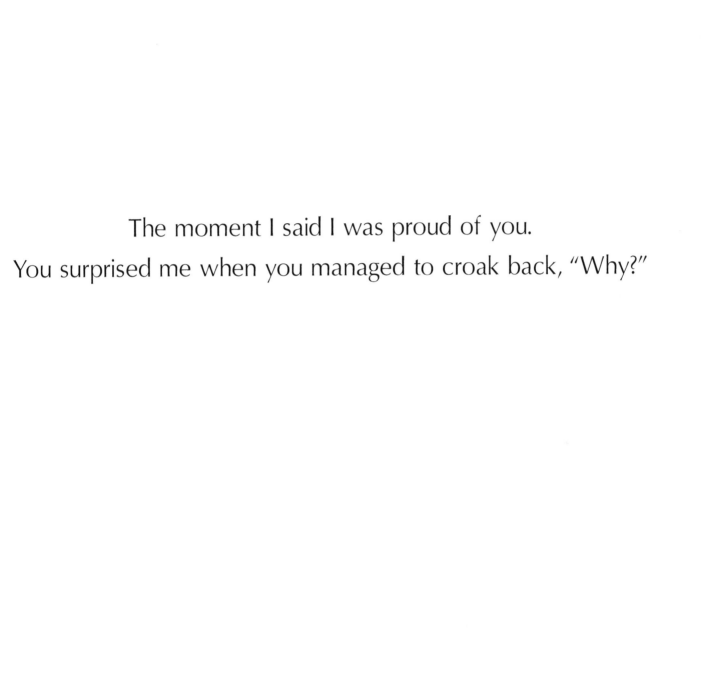

The moment I said I was proud of you.

You surprised me when you managed to croak back, "Why?"

29

The moment I surprised myself and said,
"Because I didn't think you had it in you,
this dying so well thing."
Your eyebrow went up
and you slept deeper.

30

The moment I sat alone with you
while mom stole eight minutes
to take a shower at 11:00 p.m.

31

The moments I sat by your side.
Holding your hand,
watching you breathe.
Very slowly.

32

The moments mom and I sat by your side.

Holding your hands.

Looking at each other.

Looking at you.

33

The moments I held mom's hand
while she cried.

No. 1. Thy Light is Come.

CHORUS.

A - rise, a - rise! a - rise and shine! A - rise and shine, for thy light is

The moment we broke out in song,
our voices rising to fill the room
with "You Are Mine."

35

The moments I sat by your side,
still watching you breathe.
Even more slowly.

36

The moment I whispered into your ear,
"Don't forget to say goodbye to my mom
before you go."

37

The moment you startled me
by how distinctly, clearly
and strongly you said
"I won't forget."

38

And silently. You didn't.

39

The moment you fluttered your glazing eyes
and mumbled, "She's calling me."
"Who is?"

"My mom."

40

The moments you moaned.

41

The moments we scrambled back to your side,
having only been in the kitchen to breathe.

42

The moment you whisper-croaked,
"I'm at the crossroads.
They are getting on the bus."

43

The moment I looked into mom's eyes and said, "We aren't drugging him. We are medicating him."

44

The moment she said,
"But then he might not be able
to respond to me anymore.
At all."

45

The moment I looked back at her
and said, "I know."

46

The moment I realized
we had already heard
your last words.

47

The moment I was sorry
I hadn't gotten you to
make a goodbye video
for mom.

48

The moment, sometime at 2:00 in the afternoon
on either Wednesday or Thursday,
when I realized I wouldn't trade this vigil.
This. Being here. **This.** Privilege.
For anything in the world.

49

The moment I realized
I was a death shepherd.
Yours.

50

The moment on Friday at 5:00 p.m.

the hospice nurse said

"I am worried about leaving you alone for the night."

51

The moment I noticed
your methadone and morphine,
that I carefully crushed for you,
pooling white, inside your cheek,
gently eddying.

52

The moment I had the idea
to cut a lock of your hair
at one minute past midnight
on June 13.

53

The moment I grabbed the kitchen shears,
ran back to your chair,
riffling your hair for the best piece,
saying, "I know you would have thought
to do this yourself. If it hadn't all been so fast."

54

The moment mom came around the corner
seeing me standing there with
one hand full of scissors,
the other holding your best lock.
Oh shit.

55

That moment we laughed.
Then cried.

56

That moment all I could find
was dental floss to tie it with,
your smoothest, most silver fox lock.

57

That moment she had reluctantly, finally,
closed her eyes. Strained from staring at you.
"Just for five minutes,"
she said, lying on your hospital bed,
barely an arm's length away from you.
Dead asleep.

58

You, right next to her in the red chair.

The place you wanted to die. Had to die.

Where you'd spent so much of your time.

In front of the TV.

Maddening me.

59

TV now long since switched off.
Silent.
Unmoving.
Long forgotten.

60

Her hand on your arm.

1:22 a.m.

61

That moment,
lying shoulder to shoulder with mom.
Me, just finishing an article about
"How to Know When Someone is Dying."

62

The moment I realized
I wasn't hearing you.
Hearing breathing.
Anymore.

63

I looked up.

64

"MOM!"

65

The moment we jumped up and stared.

Close.

Peering into your face.

You turning grey before our eyes.

66

The moment I saw your tongue
pushing in and out slowly,
no air moving,
as if searching for a new home.
Waving so so so slowly.
A soundless goodbye.

67

And it was.
A good.
Bye.

68

69

The moment our eyes could leave you.

We looked at the clock.

1:28 a.m.

70

The moment I realized you died better than you lived.
No fighting. Complaining none. All elegance.
Acceptance. With grace.

71

The moment I realized
I would miss you.

72

Thank you.

Joseph Costantini flew away on angel wings as gently as the wave rejoins the ocean, at 1:30 a.m., Saturday, June 13, 2020. He was 69 years old.

Joseph was born to Filippo and Rosa-Falgiani Costantini on August 9, 1950 in Aquasanta Terme, Ascoli Piceno, Italy. The family immigrated to Canada when Joseph was four years old.

Joseph met his wife Clare in 2008 on eHarmony and they had their first date at the Matagorda County Fair and Rodeo cook-off. They married on September 4, 2010 in Bay City, Texas, at Sharyl and Nate McDonald's family barn.

In addition to being a dedicated and loving father, Joseph was a well-traveled man. He was proud to say that he stepped foot on six different continents. His job took him from the rigs on the rough and cold waters of the North Sea to the dry deserts of Egypt, the Great Wall of China, the outback of Australia, the stoic Russian steppes, the shores of Scandinavia, Thailand, and Singapore, the Holy Land, Africa, the Middle East and all points between. However, the place he loved most was his sanctuary, at home with Clare in their small town of Van Vleck, Texas.

Joseph also enjoyed being a charter member and president of the Van Vleck Lions Club. He was a member of the Knights of Columbus. Joseph had an unwavering faith in God which he shared with those that surrounded him. He was very active in his church, Holy Cross Catholic Church. Joseph participated in ACTS,

That Man is You, the Holy Cross choir and the weekly Divine Mercy devotion. He was also a very proud lifetime member of the Kinsman in Ontario, Canada.

One of the jewels of Joseph's life was becoming a United States citizen in 2018.

He loved golfing with his friends, taking sunset walks on the beach with Clare and then having dinner at the Waterfront Restaurant overlooking the harbor. Joseph took great pride and satisfaction in the creation of the non-profit organization Harmony Ranch that he and Clare began in 2010. Harmony Ranch provides a safe place for those with medical, physical and/or emotional challenges to receive the empowering gift of the unconditional acceptance and support of horses.

Joseph joins his mother, Rosa, his father, Filippo, his stepmother, Amelia, who raised him and his brothers, Steve and Mario.

He is survived by his beloved Clare, his siblings in Canada: Frank Costantini and wife Loretta, Amadeo Costantini and wife Sue, Brenda Servello and husband Sam, and Phil Costantini and wife Darlene, also many loving nieces and nephews, his first wife Francine Costantini, son Christopher Costantini and wife Tara, twin daughters Rosanne Costantini and Andrea Shuster and husband Gus; also his second family: Christin Staszesky and husband Dana Harper, John Staszesky Jr. and wife Melissa, Matt Staszesky and wife Olivia, and Caitlin Saunders and wife Tiffany. He loved and delighted in his many grandchildren: Morgan, Dominic, Charlie, Mila, Maddie, Sophia, Emma, Madeline, Lilly, London, Jubilee and Paris.

He is also survived by his untold number of friends, both local and international. Joseph never met a stranger and always left one with a smile.

Joseph was a valiant warrior who found himself bravely battling cancer from the time he was 26 years old. He never allowed this vile opponent to bring him down. He kept his faith and witty humor until the very end, keeping us all in stitches even up to hours before his departure. His parting gift to us was the depth of his peacefulness as he passed.

In lieu of food or flowers, it was Joseph's last wish that donations be made to his and Clare's non-profit, Harmony Ranch. Knowing that donations would be made to Clare's work in the world of offering the gift of horses to both children and adults in need of a magical moment in time, gave a great level of tranquility and comfort to Joseph.

To all of you who supported our family in this time of saying goodbye to our dear Joseph, Houston Hospice, family and friends, you know who you are - thank you.

We will miss him greatly.

Christin Marie Staszesky
June 2020
Van Vleck, Texas

ACKNOWLEDGMENTS AND GRATITUDE

To my treasured husband Dana, for all the tea parties, kindness, endless patience and your stunning photography. Thank you. I love you.

Mom. I love you. You hadn't a clue what I was doing right under your nose. Thank you for all the 'mom-ing' you did and do for me always. I hope that holding this book in your hands, is a balm that helps to heal your heart.

My dear friend, Marsha Petter. Thank you for all the hours of praying, sitting, singing, errand running, texting, hilarity and coffee time. Our bond is cast.

To Joseph's family and especially to his three children. Chris, Rosanne and Andrea, thank you, for embracing me as family. As sister. Caring for your dad was an honor.

To Marie McComb, thank you for being our wonderfully kind hospice nurse.

Russ and Larrine Abolt, thank you for always turning me back toward my writing. It was years ago, under the alpen glow of the Swan, I claimed you as family, my very own fairy godparents. I love you guys.

To Jill Kitchen, for my paper talisman. Thank you.

Lali, puppykins, my ever constant companion. You deserve all the treats.

To the small dream team of folks I was fortunate enough to gather that helped me birth this book into being: my wildly talented, enthusiastic and gracious book designer, Mark Gelotte, my copy editor, Cass Miosic for her fast and tidy work, and my brilliant jewel of a writing teacher and developmental editor, Max Regan. Thank you. My experience of bringing a book into the world with you, has been beautiful and unforgettable.

And, finally, to you, Rosa Glenn Reilly. You already know all the words I could ever say and why. Thank you. OXOX

Christin Marie Staszesky is a poet and memoirist who lives in downtown Houston, Texas. On weekends, she can be found at Hawks Rest, her two-acre sanctuary in Van Vleck, Texas, home to five 500-year-old live oaks. She has been devoted to horses from the moment her mother took her for her first horseback ride in a corduroy blue backpack, at six weeks of age. That ride initiated her place into a family lineage of what Christin calls Horse Listeners. Into her lifetime of equine experience and partnership, she has layered, decades of experience as a yoga practitioner and teacher and is now a respected Gestaltist. Christin's private practice weaves the gifts of equine medicine with Gestalt psychology, neuroscience and somatic wisdom. Christin identifies the Light Rider as her own personal archetype, passionately traveling, without apology, the shadowed and luminous richness of the spectrum of life. She is also an amazing soup maker, beachcomber and stargazer.

www.thelightrider.com

christin@thelightrider.com